The Dream
A Short History
Of WCTC

By

Jack Shreve
Dominic Santora

Tony DeNicola

Editor

Hard Knocks Publishing

Prefaces

The dream started in the forties, and in the eighties, Jack Shreve had a vision of writing the history of this historic radio station, but it took another forty years before that dream was accomplished. Jack set forth the foundation, and what we tried to accomplish was filling in the gap between 1982 to the present, which included personal testimonials from past employees and newspaper articles to take you along this magical ride that started in 1948.

Forward

Only the dream will last.

Some distant day

The wheels will falter,

and the Silent sun

Will see the last beam leveled to

And all men's futile clangor spent

And done.

Yet after brick and steel and

Stone are gone,

And flesh and blood are duet, the

Dream lives on.

Sonnet – Only the Dream is Real - - Anderson Seugge

The purpose of the brief history of WCTC was gleaned from various sources, including the memories of several persons whose interest in the project was incited by the idea that it would be fun to remember the past.

It is far from a detailed historical story that was not meant to be all-inclusive. It skims over periods, from one person to thank you for believing in me when I needed encouragement.

Jack Shreve

The Dream

When WCTC went on air on December 12, 1946, it culminated in several years of hard work by several people involved in the planning and development held by James Howe. He was responsible for putting Radio Station WCTC on the air in New Brunswick, New Jersey.

After graduating from Rutgers University in the early 1930s, Howe went to work for a radio station in Virginia, where he eventually rose to the position of General Manager. When the United States entered the war in 1941, How joined the service, serving the honors. At the end of the war in 1946, Howe returned home, where his interest in broadcasting continued and eventually led him to discuss the possibility of starting his radio station. He contacted several fellow Rutgers graduates who encouraged him to seek a station in New Brunswick. The idea appealed to Howe, and he began bringing the dream to fruition.

Approval for a transmitter site on the banks of the Raritan River in Highland Park came in August of 1948, and plans began taking shape to put WCTC AM on the air. It would be a 250-watt, full-time station at 1450 on the dial.

Bankers were found, a company was formed, and Howe's dream began to shape. He called on those loyal friends of Rutgers with whom he had been so long associated, and together they started the task. First plans called for the station to go on air in September 1946, but delays forced postponements to October and then December. Howe called the company the Chanticleer Broadcasting Company," named after the mascot of Rutgers University. He said WCTC call letters didn't stand for anything in particular but were the closest he could get to C-B-C; Howe was named President and General Manager of WCTC.

The other members of the company's Board of Directors were:

Emil F. Klein, Alexander Ungar, Inc.

Duke S. Leonard, Squibb Laboratories

John A. Lynch, Counsellor at Law

James Maher, Maher Funeral Home

Louis Migliorini, Rutgers Chevrolet

Kenneth Perry, Johnson & Johnson

W. Burton Salisbury, O'Connell & Salisbury

Juan Sanchez, National Bank of New Jersey

Ernest H. Webb, Webb Wire Works.

Those who were hired to run the radio station:

Station Manager: James Howe, Air Corps, U.S. Army

Sales Manager: Ed Derryberry, Air Corps, U.S. Army

Assistant Sales

Manager: Frank Weingart, American Red Cross

Chief Engineer: Bob Williams, U.S. Navy

Engineer: John Ward, Infantry, U.S. Army

Program Director: Jerry Baker, Infantry, U.S. Army

New Director: Mike Germak, Signal Corps, U.S. Army

Announcers: Bob Bell, Infantry, U.S. Army

Joe Helgeson, Infantry, U.S. Army

Gerry Weeden, Air Corps, U.S. Army

Community Writers: Dick Mercer, U.S. Navy

                      Thelma Enoch

Secretary: Edith Howe

Soon the kinks that always go along with putting a station on the air were worked out, and the dream was about to be realized.

Thursday, December 12, 1946, arrived. It was 6:10 a.m. when the transmitter carrier was put in the "on" position. The engineers running test programming all week decided to adjust, and the transmitter was turned off at 6:15 a.m. Thirty seconds later, it was turned back on. At 6:30 a.m., the programming began from the third floor of the Peoples National Bank on Georges Street in New Brunswick. WCTC was on the air, and the dream of James Howe was realized.

The First Days

The programming on that first day in December 1946 was innovative, to say the least. Through a flurry of newspaper ads, Howe had promised New Brunswick and Middlesex County residents that WCTC would be a local station, and he kept this promise.

The music was laid back, by today's standards, with such program titles as "Record Reveille," "Music Without Words," "Mid-Day Music," and "Sunnyside and Lean Back Music." On the other hand, public service programming was innovative. It included "Let's Go Visiting," where an announcer would take a wire recorder into the streets to have residents respond with their opinions.

The first commercial aired on WCTC came at 7:00 a.m. and was for the New Brunswick Roofing Works. Commercials followed it for J.J. Fisch, Budd Jewelers, Rivoli Pipe Shop, and the 7:45 a.m. News was sponsored by the New Brunswick Savings Bank, which continued to sponsor that newscast for many years. Some other companies that stayed with WCTC over the years include Jersey Tire, Freeze Camera Shop, and the House of Fashion.

WCTC stressed local involvement in its programming and, according to newspaper clippings, received praise from many local communities for broadcasting News of interest to them.

The first tape-delayed broadcast appears to have been in March of 1947, when the dinner of the Plainfield Jaycees was recorded and played back later in the day. The first play-by-play of a sporting event occurred during the 1947 basketball season when WCTC broadcasted the sectional finals of local high schools at the Rutgers College Avenue gym, New Brunswick, St. Peter's, Highland Park, South Brunswick, and Sayreville High Schools were involved. The first game is believed to have been between Highland Park and Flemington on March 5, followed by a second game between New Brunswick and Plainfield. They were done live by the WCTC sports crew, including Bob Bell, Ed Isaacs, and Gordon McCoy.

The first delayed broadcast of a high school basketball game came on March 27 when WCTC recorded the St. Peter's encounter with LaSalle College High School of Philadelphia and rebroadcast it at 6:30 that evening.

WCTC Broadcast its first parade on Memorial Day 1947 from Woodbridge and its first high school band concert on March 28, 1947.

An open house was held at the WCTC studios in New Brunswick on February 19. So, as the first year ended, the Station had grown into a community-minded facility that saw such programs as community news aired several times a day. That tradition continued into the eighties when 4:30 p.m. Somerset County News was still being broadcast.

Traffic reports, live church broadcasts, remotes, play-by-play, and the top-rated Rutgers football coach, "The Harvey Harmon Show," heard each Friday night, made up the seventeen-hour broadcasting day. WCTC was on the air daily from 6:00 a.m. to 11:00 p.m. and on Sunday from 8:00 a.m. to 11:00 p.m.

From 1946 through 1950, the Station continued to flourish. But James Howe, who continued to run the ship, wasn't one to a standstill. He began proceedings to get another station and, In August of 1947, was granted a license to build an FM radio station. By the end of the first broadcast year, WCTC's staff was 65 percent Rutgers University graduates. As with all radio stations, there are changes in the staff. The names changed over the years, but the principal objective of James Howe continued to prevail.

The first News Department consisted of John Schiller, Don Meany, and Barney Ryan. Ryan took over as head of the News Department in 1948. The first traffic report was aired in 1947, and WCTC began broadcasting school closings during bad weather.

At this time, WCTC began airing a new program to bring a much-needed outlet to the large New Brunswick Hungarian population.

It was called "Kara's Hungarian Melody Time," and It became an instant hit with the public.

On September 9, 1948, WCTC-FM went on air, broadcasting sixteen hours daily.

Bob Bell became Program Director in 1948 and headed a staff that included Mike Siman in Sports, Lee Rose, John Schiller in News, Jack Gleason, Same Christopher, and a roving reporter named Herb Kaplow.

Another young man who worked for WCTC in those early days was Nat Shoewalter.

In 1949 a group of New Jersey radio stations got together and decided to send a reporter overseas to interview local military men and feed the tapes back for air. Herb Kaplow was that reporter, and he reported back on short wave. In September 0f 1949, Kaplow represented eighteen New Jersey stations.

Growing Pains

"THINK NEWS WHILE IT'S NEWS"

That sign hung in the WCTC News Room in 1950, and it depicted the ideals of the entire operation of the Station.

As the fourth anniversary approached, the commitment to community involvement was never more prevalent.

Mighty Mike was introduced in September 1950 as the new mascot of WCTC, replacing Rooster. The Station was a member of the Garden State Network, a group of stations whose idea was to cover News throughout the state on a cooperative basis. The other stations included WNCR Newark, WTTM Trenton, WKDN Camden, WJLK Asbury Park, WFPG Atlantic City, and WSNJ Bridgeton.

These stations covered the 1950 elections together, a huge success.

WCTC published a newspaper in 1950 called "The Listening Post," and there was a brief story about the Sports Department like this: Tony Marano is behind the scene as the guiding hand of sportscasters. His job is to contact hundreds of correspondents, translate the information into concise, accurate, and readable copy, and finally, put it on the air. At 10:30 p.m., he has twenty minutes to prepare the information for the News.

Tony came to WCTC in June of 1949 as a part-time news writer. In September of 1950, he was a Sports Editor.

Some of his early interviews were with Don Newcombe, Jim Braddock, and Tom Janiro.

Barbara Bowers had risen to Assistant Program Director in November 1950, and Don Meaney was still in charge of Programming.

Some other names that might bring back memories of those early, growing years include Ken Leslie and Bod Jordan, who took over the early morning "Yawn Patrol." Charles Creager was an engineer, and Ken Bernstein, Tony Marano, and Joe Dembo were newsmen.

Billed as "The Largest News Staff in the State," they covered a fire in 1947 at the First Presbyterian Church on Church Street and the South Amboy fire in 1950.

WCTC was on the air from the Middlesex County Fair in 1950 with their mid-morning, all-star team of Barbara and Joe. The Barbara was Mrs. Moreno Bauer, and Joe was Joe Dembo. News Chief in that year was Ralph Mahoney, and Lino Harmer, Arnie Brooks, and Jack Allen were staff announcers.

Programming that year included a musical interlude for shut-ins and a continued flow of sports, with Bob Bell still leading the play-by-play crew, including Dave Moss and Tony Marano.

1953

By 1953, WCTC, now approaching its seventh year as the "Voice of Central Jersey," continued to grow. James Howe, the driving force behind the Station, was still President of the Chanticleer Broadcasting Company but had relinquished some leadership by naming Robert Williams as Manager of the Station. Howe was, at this time, deeply involved in the operation of the Company's newly acquired Station, WIRA, in Fort Pierce, Florida.

WCTC and WCTC-FM continued to flourish, and the Station, founded on the principle of "Community Service to Central New Jersey," was still presenting programs in the public interest – "It's So Good to Be with You" with Milt Cowen on WCTC's daily Farm Bulletin, and "United Fund," adventures in research.

James Vogdes headed the sales staff of three. Victor Takach was Chief Engineer, and Barbara Bauer had risen to the rank of Program Director. Tony Marano led the Sports and News Departments, including Ed Mack, Garcin Kaganowich, and Leroy Smith.

The other staff members' names included John Molnar, Ray Honda, and Joe Lovaez in Engineering; Carol Crazy and Martha Gramnese, office staff; and Tom Dowd, Moss Rose, Jack Allen, and Paul L. Smith, announcers.

By 1953 many of the pioneer broadcasters had left WCTC for greener pastures. In a booklet published by WCTC in August of 1953 for its public, the Station's mascot, "Mighty Mike," reminisced about the alumni.

Bob Bell had entered the motion picture business; Ken Bernstein joined the Army; Arnie Brooks (Zucker) went to Rutgers in the Public Relations Department, and Pat Cappacio became Editor with the Rahway Record.   Joe Dembo joined NBC News; Jack Dentz moved over to Rutgers in the TV/Public Relations Department; Bob Drews migrated to WAAF in Chicago; Gerry Ennis joined the U.S. Air Force; Jack Gleason went to work for WAAT in Newark; and Tom Gregory was an announcer at WPAT in Paterson. Harvey Hauptman was in the Army but was expected to return in November, while John P. Jones was on the TV staff of WABS-TV; Herb Kaplow was a newsman at WRC in Washington, D.C.; Roland Kelly moved to sales at WSBT in Indiana; Milt Lederman was a PR Director for the New Brunswick United Fund. Ed Locke went to work as the morning man at WIP in Philadelphia, and Don Meaney was at NBC News in New York. Dick Mercer wrote copy for an advertising agency in New York; Dave Mose was Program Director at WESC in South Carolina, while Nat Shoehalter, who had been with WATV in Newark, returned to Rutgers University's Public Relations Department. Danny Stiles was an announcer with WVNJ in Newark.

1956

Two events in 1956 stand out as a tribute to WCTC's dedication to serving the public. In the early hours of February 16, a fire of undetermined origin broke out at the transmitter site in Highland Park. It destroyed the ability of WCTC to broadcast that day. But, through the engineering staff's diligence and the management's quick action, WCTC was back on the air by 7:35 that night.

At 7:35 p.m. on the 16th, WCTC used the facilities of Pillar of Fire Station WAWZ in Zarepath, Franklin Township. In a newspaper story about the fire, estimated to have cost thirty thousand dollars of damages, WCTC Engineers quickly purchased a new AM transmitter and, working through the night, had the Station back on the air by 6:30 the following day. It was some time before the FM transmitter was replaced and the Station returned on the air.

The second event 0f 1956 was the invasion of Hungary by the Russians.
More than a thousand miles away, this event proved to be another of the many in which WCTC could lend its facilities to the community in a time of need.

Having one of the most prominent Hungarian communities outside the homeland, New Brunswick became the focal point of the refuge's "Flight to Freedom" operation. WCTC, besides providing updated information about the birthplace of many of its Hungarian listeners, got deeply involved in the community's need for data about the refugee problem that was growing at Camp Kilmer, where many of the fleeing Hungarians were arriving daily. Public service programming on the situation was broadcast daily to help the community in its need to know what was going on both at home and abroad.

In retrospect, this was one of the many reasons why WCTC Radio became one of the community's most respected members. WCTC was able to communicate with the community.

The Sixties

The sixties for WCTC were a decade of an experiment. Many pioneers who forged WCTC's image were replaced by a new breed of broadcasters. The new owners, who were just as dedicated as James Howe to serving the local community, began to refine the programming. Fresh ideas, new directions, innovative programming, and new professionalism took over. But even with this approach, the theme established in 1946 by James Howe of the community
service remained.

Both Joseph Rosenmiller and Peter Bordes were enthusiastic and dedicated radio broadcasters and took a personal interest in the building of the Station. They both took an active role in the running of the Station and hired several new people, and established a new set of station policies that, in years to come, would prove to make WCTC even better than before.

They elevated Tony Marano to Assistant General Manager and began working with him to move him up to lead the Station.

They hired experienced radio people to bring new ideas and fresh approaches into the broadcasting business.

Some of those who joined the Station in the early part of the decade included Jack Ham, who went on to become an administrative assistant, Jack Ellery took over for Cliff Haycock as morning man in late 1962; Jack Shreve, who worked closely with management in the area of programming and special events, Bob Huse became Production Director and eventually Program Director, and set a new high in commercial production. Julian Breen, a college student at Rutgers, came to WCTC in the mid-sixties and worked on special projects. After Tom Moran left for WIP in Philadelphia, Mike Frantinuno (Mike Jay) joined the announcing staff. John Taylor and a host of other announcers followed him.

News and Sports were still under the direction of Tony Marano, and Art Mackwell was named in 1962 to News Director. During the early sixties, WCTC covered serval national news stories. During the Mercury sub-orbital and outer-space flights, America's first venture into space was given 24-hour coverage. This was done locally, as WCTC had no network affiliation. The disastrous assassination of President Kennedy in 1963 was covered locally from beginning to end, with the local news department manning the air continually through the funeral.

The local news was not neglected, and the New Brunswick, Plainfield, and Newark riots were given on-the-spot coverage in much the same way news was covered in the early days.

Sports coverage continued to be a staple of the broadcasting day on WCTC in the sixties, with the Station airing many games in which two high school-level superstars played their talent. John Somoygi of St. Peter's in New Brunswick was busy setting a state record of 3,310 points in a career carrying his team to the state championship. Meanwhile, Brian Taylor of Perth Amboy led the Panthers in the same direction with his superb play. The two superstars never met in a high school play but did meet once. That occurred in Jadwin Gym when Taylor was leading Princeton, and Somoygi transferred from New Mexico to Rutgers. And WCTC was there to cover the confrontation as it had been for many years.

When Rutgers basketball fortunes returned, so did WCTC's coverage, with Bill Foster leading All-American Bob Lloyd and Jim Valvano into the first NIT.

Again, Tony Marano and WCTC were there to cover the action.

WCTC made significant gains in the sixties under the direction of Tony and the new owners, and plans were afoot to move the Station into new facilities.

WCTC had begun to outgrow the third floor of the Peoples National Bank. The staff increased to nearly forty employees, and workers generally shared a desk.

There were many great moments for the staff and management during the sixties. Virgil Scudder became News Director, leading the team through the decade's end, continuing to foster the high standards set by his predecessors. When Scudder left for New York and WINS, Ed Scott, a seasoned veteran, became News Director and named Jack Shreve as his assistant.

WCTC expanded its broadcasting day from 5:30 a.m. to 5:00 a.m. during the sixties. The announcer lineup was stabilized, with Jack Ellery becoming a morning institution with his wit and professionalism. He was followed by Mike Jay, John Taylor, and Bob Huse, with Bob Tarring in the evening. By the decade's end, the seasoned staff had many years of experience and kept pace with the original WCTC ideal of community service.

In the News Department during the sixties, such names as Harry Hart, Roger Cohen, Jack Shreve, Tom LaCue, Paul Springle, and a host of others carried on the tradition in the seventies for WCTC News as the top broadcasting team in the state.

The Seventies

The names changed, and the policies became more precise. Still, WCTC in the seventies continued to thrive and grow, and probably because of the nucleus of the leadership, it kept the perspective of community service to Central New Jersey as its aim.

Tony Marano was in complete command, and the owners had moved on to other ventures, buying other stations and creating a corporation called Greater Media.

In the seventies, the staff grew, and it became more and more apparent that new facilities would have to be found soon.

Under the leadership of Bob Huse, Mike Jay, and John Taylor, the announcing staff remained intact in the early decade. Huse left first, and then Mike Jay moved to another station in the Midwest. Taylor went onto WVNY, and long-time announcer Dean Hunter was hired. Ellery, Shreve, and Michael Jarmus were still around, and Bob Thomas was added to the staff. Programming changed a little in the seventies but maintained the professionalism it had always had. The news came under the leadership of Walt Sodie, and the staff included such names as Lee Shirvanian, Jack Shreve, Ralph Saro, Shelly Stricker, and a host of others. Coverage of local news never suffered and instead increased. Floods, fires, explosions, legislative elections, town meetings, community parades, and national news were publicly covered.

And with the addition of the Associated Press Radio Network, the world was at Central Jersey's fingertips.

The sales staff, traffic, copy, and production departments kept pace, and business boomed.

As the decade ended, WCTC and WCTC-FM, now called WQMR, engaged in one of the most critical events. After years of delay and problems, the ground was broken for the new facilities on Veronica Avenue in Somerset. WQMR changed its call letter to WMGQ and split away. Both stations moved into the new facilities in 1978 and continued to provide Central Jersey with music and information. The decade ended on a high note with the tradition still intact. WCTC and WMGQ…the heart and sound of Central New Jersey.

The Eighties

In the 1980s, WCTC continued to be guided by Tony Marano as Vice President of Greater Media and General Manager of WCTC and WMGQ.

The key members of the WCTC staff included Ellery, Shreve, Jarmus, Renee Kancylarz, Paul Berlin, Clarence Dingman, Ed Meirose, Harry Mitchell, Walt Sodie, and Jo Ann Nolan. These people had a total of over 150 years of service among them.

Ellery and Shreve joined WCTC in the early sixties; Jarmus, while at Rutgers, joined the staff, left for the Vietnam conflict, and returned after his service stint. Renee began her career in the office, left, and then returned to become an Administrative Assistant. Berlin and Meirose, a salesman from the fifties, were still doing their thing. Dingman, who began in the fifties at WCTC and rose to Chief Engineer, was instrumental in planning the new facilities.

As Sales Manager and Sodie as News Director, Mitchell rounded out the nucleus of the critical staff members who have led WCTC into the eighties.

What the future holds for WCTC is anyone's guess, but if the history is to be of any benefit, the ideal set forth by James Howe when he formulated the idea for WCTC in 1946 in a newspaper as if December 10, 1946, "WHAT MAKES WCTC DIFFERENT THAN ANY OTHER RADIO STATION ON YOUR DAIL?" Briefly, WCTC is the only radio station dedicated exclusively to the interest of New Brunswick and Middlesex County and consistently broadcasts events of interest to the area's people.

That has expanded to include Somerset County, but the idea remains.

Author's Notes

It would have been impossible to complete this brief outline of WCTC's history without the cooperation of those former and present employees whose memories span from when James Howe first began his project in 1946.

In checking, I found several early radio pioneers who were quite interested in my project and were very helpful in checking my facts and giving me ideas on new areas to cover in this outline. I am grateful to Arnie Zucker, Nat Shoehalter, and Dick Lewis for their memories of the early WCTC history. The host of the present employees was also helpful for their patience. They included Jo Ann Nolan, Mary Jackes, Renee Kancylarz, Ed Meirose, and Clarence Dingman.

This brief history was not to be an in-depth study of local radio or an all-encompassing chronicle, although it could have included more memories with a bit more digging. At one point, I wanted to include brief biographical sketches and the names of all those who contributed to WCTC's history. However, time and space limits prevented me from making this happen in a large volume.

My only hope is that those who scan its contents will be prouder of being associated with their fellow workers and take pride in the men and women who went before them to pursue sound broadcasting.

Jack Milton Shreve

Sketches

James Howe, one of the founders of the New Jersey Broadcasters Association, passed away on November 7, 1979, in St. Petersburgh, Florida. Mr. Howe was a Rutgers graduate who became an Air Force Major after World War II. He was sixty-nine. He owned and operated WCTC Radio in New Brunswick until 1956.

Anthony Marano began his broadcasting career at WCTC in 1949 as a sports reporter. He soon became Sports Director and would hold the positions of New Director, Assistant Station Manager, and General Manager in the coming years. In 1982 "Tony" was Vice President of Greater Media, the parent company, and continued to lead the staff of WCTC as General Manager. In 1981 Marano retired from one of his loves – "Broadcasting Rutgers football and basketball" – which he had done for thirty years.

Arnie Zucker joined WCTC in January 1950 as a morning man. He stayed with the station for two-and-a-half years until 1952. During that time, he worked various air shifts and held Chief Announcer and Acting Program Director positions. In 1982 Arnie was the Executive Director of the New Jersey Broadcasters Association.

Nat Shoehalter joined WCTC on its first broadcast day in 1950. After holding various positions, Nat left the station and went to work for Rutgers University, where he was still employed in 1982.

In the early days, Richard Lewis became a staff member and, while staying only a short time at WCTC, moved on to WJLK in Asbury Park, New Jersey, where he is still heard today. His magnetic voice has made him one of the most delightful contributions to radio in the Garden State.

Edward Meirose joined WCTC as a salesman in 1955 and continues in that position.

Paul Berlin joined WCTC in 1959 as a salesman and was named Assistant General Manager in the 1970s.

Clarence Dingman joined WCTC in the early days as an engineer, rose to the position of Chief Engineer, and when WCTC and WMGQ split, he was named Chief Engineer of WCTC.

The deceased Alice Rose held the position of Record Librarian for many years and was responsible for the filing system still in use today.

Jack Ellery (Eisner) came to WCTC in December 1962 as the morning man. He continues in that capacity even today.

<u>News Directors</u>

From the early New Directors mentioned in this book to the present time, WCTC has been regarded as one of the most delicate news operations in the country. Many "graduates" have gone on to larger and more responsible situations in various parts of the country.

Tony Marano held the position for many years. Still, because of management responsibilities, they finally relinquished it to Art Mackwell after Mackwell left in the early sixties—Virgil Scudder, Ed Scott, and Walt Sodie.

It would be impossible to name all of those fine newsmen and women who have gone through the WCTC News Department over the years, but to name a few – Art Brown, who went on to WABC Sports; Mike Ludlum, WCBS Radio; Shelly Strickler, WOR News; as well as Phil Painter, Fred Fishkin, Tom LaCue and Lee Shirvanian.

Renee Kancylarz joined WCTC in the early sixties and currently holds the position of Administrative Assistant to General Manager.

Jo Ann Nolan joined WCTC in the sixties and is now the Traffic Manager responsible for the daily log.

Michael Jarmus joined WCTC while still a student at Rutgers in the late sixties. After a stint in the service, he returned to the station to become an announcer and Public Service Director.

Jack Shreve, an announcer, Music Director, joined WCTC in 1961 in Programming, switched to News in the mid-sixties, and returned to the air in 1974 as host of the popular show, "WCTC Remembers."

<u>Program Directors</u>

Aside from those mentioned in the other section of this history – Harvey Hauptman held the position of Program Director for a decade leaving in the late 1950s. He was succeeded by Bob Huse, Mike Jay, John Taylor, Dean Hunter, Jack Ellery, and Jay Meyers.

Other Contributors

Harry Mitchell, Sales Manager

George Boyler, Salesman

Andy Schnatter, Salesman

John Stanley, Engineer

Robert Tarring, Announcer

Danny Stiles, Announcer

Julian Brean, Announcer, Administrator

Larry Berger, Traffic, Announcer

David Marish, News, Announcer

Roger Cohen, News, and Sports

David Moss, Announcer

Phil Painter, News

Tom Moran, Announcer

Ron Peters Engineer

Bill Price, Copy

Ed Spiegel, Copy

Mary Jacques, Traffic

Barbara Weiss, Traffic

Susan Miskoff, Copy

Joan McClure, Administrator

Ron Miskoff, Announcer

...And Now the Unmentioned Generation

Gary Rnel

It was in the mid-'90s when I was able to secure a position at WCTC. Well, I actually secured two positions if I wanted a full-time job. I am a native of Central Jersey and, at the time, was working at an all-news station in Springfield, Massachusetts, following my first radio gig in the Hartford market. GM, Tony Marano, said that if I worked with Walt Sodie in the newsroom and did an air shift, he would combine the two positions to create a full-time job.

There was no hesitation on my part. WCTC was one of America's greatest, most respected local radio stations at the time. Plus, I wanted to return to New Jersey. Working in the illustrious and award-winning newsroom was indeed a great experience. Sadly, these newsrooms no longer exist today except in significant market news and talk stations.

PD, Jay Meyers, offered me the opportunity to do a talk shift at the station, and from there, as they say, the rest is history. I worked in New York City as a News Director and Talk Show Host, as well as Talk Radio in Philadelphia.

Jack Ellery was my mentor. I grew up listening to Jack, hoping to hear him say one thing. "Woodbridge Township schools are closed for the day." Jack was an extraordinary talent. After college, I attended the first class of the "Jack Ellery School of Broadcasting" and learned a great deal about the industry and honed my skills as a broadcaster.

WCTC has spawned many significant talents in the radio industry, and I was extremely fortunate to spend the early years of my career working with talented professionals.

Dominic Santora

I remember hearing those call letters WCTC when I graduated from the Allen/Singer School of Broadcasting. Bill Singer, the school owner, and operator worked with Tony Marano back in the day, and Mr. Marano would use the school to pull young talent to start their journey in broadcasting. So, he was looking for someone to work on the remote crew, and Singer felt it was a good fit since I ran my own mobile DJ company. I figured it would be fun but didn't realize what I was getting into.

The first day I walked into the lobby, I felt like I was in a New York radio station, not Somerset, NJ. I thought I was in over my head, but when I meant Jack, and he introduced me to some of the on-air staff, I started to relax. This station had hundreds of years of experience, but their ego was left for the air.

After walking me around the station, Jack turned to me and asked, "So when can you start?" " We went over my availability, and he warned me that if you go out with this particular talent, make sure you know where the payphones are because you'll find him there. I started laughing; the first time I did a remote with this guy, I became nervous when he vanished 20 minutes before the remote started. The station wanted microphone checks with the talent's voice, not mine. I took a walk around the venue and found him. He looked at me like I was bothering him and asked, WHAT? I replied that the control room wanted you off the phone and needed a level check.

I learned that you must be strong and direct the talent, or it will run over you. On the other hand, the producer must keep professionalism fluent. I liked doing the live remotes, which lasted less than six months.

Jack pulled me into the studio to work with Don Smith, the production manager; he was my mentor. I would fill in for Don when he was off work and enjoyed this business side. I would be in the studio with Don and absorb his tricks and knowledge, but I was in charge when that first day came; I nearly crapped my pants.
I remember the first time I was working with Bruce Johnson; he hosted the Bob Reasso show, which featured a couple of his players, including Lexi Lalas. I was about halfway through the show and noticed

the lights were blinking. Now, I had to stop the show and develop a technical excuse. I told them we had a bad tape and needed to restart. The coach and the players gave me a dirty look, but Bruce being the professional he was, just said let me know when you're ready. I told Bruce what happened, and after that day, for years later, out of the blue, Bruce would ask we are taping?

The best part of working at WCTC was that you could make and grow from mistakes. Also, you learn to have a thick skin because they won't let you forget about those times either.

I was in production for about a few months, and Jack approached me and asked if I wanted to move up to the major leagues. He told me we were changing the format and needed a board op for the morning show; the host will be Jack Ellery. This guy was a legend, and I never ran a live board before. Jack told me I didn't have to worry. All you have to do is hit the button, and there will be executive produce to book guess and reach out on breaking news stories.

What do I have to lose? Either climb my way up the ladder or end a short career in radio. Working with Jack was a once-in-a-lifetime experience. He took me under his wing, and I learned a lot from him, which I passed on during my career to others breaking into the business. One of the standout highlights was when we covered the Kermit the Frog and Miss Piggy breakup. We had Kermit, and Missy Piggy was on Good Morning America. I remember telling Jack over the talkback to look at the TV, and there she was, sitting on a couch, telling the world she and Kermit were over. The best part was that we were the only media outlet to have Kermit.

Jack saw the hotline and told me to find out the stipulations of the interview. I relayed the rules and told Jack he would only talk to Kermit the Frog, and Mr. Henson was too busy to come on the air. In Jack's fashion, he blasted WTF; he is Kermit the Frog. During the interview, Jack goes through the talkback, "Hey kid, you can do a better Kermit than him." We didn't know and discovered over the weekend that Jim Henson was sick and died. We were the only station to have his last interview.

After six months into the show, our Executive Producer, Ruth Ann, was left, which was my end. I remember getting called into Mr. Marano's office on a Friday after the show; I thought this wouldn't be good. Mr. Marano sat me down and said, but I learned Tony d we would change things up for the morning show, and Jack is bringing in his old producer from Philly. I asked, so this is it, and Mr. Marano said yes for the morning show but not for the station. He continued, saying, If I have talent, I reshuffle them; I don't get rid of them. At the time, we were doing the Nutra System promotion, and he said plus, you can stay on the promotion and continue to lose weight.

I always feared going into that office; like a little kid going into the principal's office, I learned it was all about respect, and we were a family besides being a business. I went back to production, worked on sports broadcasts, and later produced all the Rutgers University coaches and post shows.

A funny story during this time, I was hired to work at another station, and Jack Shreve needed a favor; two weeks prior, I told Jack I couldn't work at CTC anymore because the other station saw it as a conflict of interest. Anyway, Jack asked if I could do this Saturday shift, and later that night, we were going to simulcast the Fourth of July fireworks; he convinced me you wouldn't have to go on air, and someone would cover the show.

A four-hour shift turned into 6, 8, into 12 hours. The person that was scheduled did not show up or call. I saw Tony Dee come in and told him I was in a bind and asked if he could do all the throw-overs and element intros, and of course, he did. All I have to do is hit play when the fireworks are ready, or so I thought. I got a call from the site to do a soundcheck, and of course, I was getting the shot called, but it wasn't going over the phone line. They told me no problem when I hear the standby and fire, say it over the phone, and try to say it before I hear it.

It's showtime, and everything is going flawlessly; we hit the finale, and the cymbal crash sank perfectly with the explosions; I never get excited over fireworks, but I let out a big WOW. The best part of the story was when I went to work at the other station; my Program Director told me how impressed he was and how the simulcast and fireworks were flawless, only if he knew. The voice on the phone said, "Easy big boy, we're not done yet."

I ended up leaving that station and picked up more hours at CTC. In all, I did three stints with Jack in the morning. I left the station in 94 and moved to Las Vegas to work for a sports network. After a year, I was ready to come home and called Jack Shreve. Before I told him I was coming back home, he asked if I could start in 3 weeks. Jack would call me weekly, saying I got you on the schedule. I worked at night on a couple of live shows and network programming. I enjoyed this shift because I was exposed to beginning the technique producer for the Rutgers Coaches shows. Plus, I was involved in the Saturday Morning programming, including the Great Central Jersey Garage Sale and Asked the Doctor.

One Saturday, I had the surprise of my life. The hotline rang, and I wondered what I did do. It was Mr. Marano, at this time, when I was gone, he retired; I asked how I could help you, and he replied, I was calling for you. I heard you are back in school, and I'm proud you are staying on target for your goals. That's what kind of leader he was, and before he hung up, he said Dominic, you can call me Tony.

I stood on until 2000 when I graduated from college and later returned to school to obtain a dual master's. Currently, I am a special education teacher.

Dan (Wota) Walker

I was at WCTC/WMGQ for about seven years, and for all of those seven years.

I followed Jack Shreve. He would hang back for those few minutes of the transition from his show to the 15-minute news block at 10:45, leading into my show at 11.

He was always helpful and generous with his comments, updates about the station, etc. Although I was a long-haired, bearded bad boy, he seemingly never held it against me & maybe at best tolerated it by young upstart ways; but while he may have been direct at times, he was never mean-spirited. I truly believe he loved WCTC & wanted it to be appreciated.

I had no idea that he ever listened to my show at all until one night when he told me that he had been listening & was willing to offer some

pointers.

Tony (Dee) DeNicola

I was hired at WCTC in August of 1976, I was 22 years old when I applied after graduating from broadcasting school, but I was rejected due to my lack of experience. So, I received some experience and was hired by WFNV 106.3 in Blairstown, NJ. 30 years later; I became the chief engineer of WFMV under Clear Channel Communications, now iHeart Media. After getting my feet wet in Blairstown. Tony Marano hired me after some influence From my father, who went to school with Tony, and my uncle, who knew the news director Walt Sodie. At the time, Dean Hunter was the program director and was the one who hired me.

I began working at WCTC when it was on top of the Peoples National Bank in New Brunswick; it was a great experience to work there growing up with the radio station. I started doing an hour between 1 and 2 am, being trained by the overnight announcer Ed Ronan. After that, I started doing 11 to 2 am shifts, and following my shift, we would sign off the air for that day's programming.

One of the things I remember is that one night Jack Shreve asked me to fill in for him because the word around the station was that I sounded very similar to Jack on the air. So, one night, Jack needed to leave his shift early, and he didn't want to say anything to the higher-ups and asked me if I could come in an hour early to cover his last hour and pretend I was him. So, I went on air saying I was him, and Jack left me $2.75 in an envelope to cover for him, which was the going rate at the time. I will never forget that moment.

Jack was a great guy, and I genuinely miss him. I always filled in for Jack on his WCTC Remembers program, which ran from 7:15 to 10:45 on weeknights.

As time passed, I got my show on Saturday nights, from 6 pm to 12 am. I was the last person to sign off the station at 385 George Street on top of the Peoples National Bank in New Brunswick at midnight on a

Sunday. The next day we signed on at our new offices and studios on Veronica Avenue. I was also part of the engineering staff, with chief engineer John Stanley and his crew that built all the new studios. Not only was I a disc jockey, but I was also a part of the engineering team. I remember one day during a Rutgers game when the transmitter was burning up at the Highland Park site. I was called in to babysit the site while John Stanley went to Camden to pick up a new transformer for the AM transmitter. Tony Marano didn't want to shut the station down because there was a Rutgers game on the air, so I had a fan blowing on the transmitter transformer to keep it cool while I was taking in toxic flumes as it was burning up.

I remember working with Elliot Stifel, Dan Flatt, and so many people who passed on, like Jack Shreve, Jack Ellery, Bernie Goydish, and Pete Kara. I was their engineer on Sunday afternoons. I also called in to save the Jack Ellery Show when they purchased a jingle package, and no one knew to use them correctly. They knew I had a Tony Dee shout and how to work the jingles into the show. So in return, I was hired to be Ellery's producer in the morning to work on those jingles and his show.

I also remember when Jack Ellery became the program director, had a broadcasting school and fired me for reasons besides not liking my Tony Dee Jingle to put someone on the air who went to his school.

Six months later, the phone rang as I came into the house from food shopping with my wife, and to my surprise, it was Ellery asking how she would like her old job back.

First, he answered Ellery here, and I responded, " Hi, Jack, what's up, he then asked if I would like my old show back.

I responded what do you mean? He repeated your old show back. Would you like to come back? I was taken aback and told Jack it'd been a long and I didn't know. When would you want back? He responded, RIGHT NOW. He continued to say it's either you or me, and I don't know what to do for WCTC Remembers. I said under one condition: you don't bother me and let me do my own thing.

I told Jack I would get there as soon as possible I just got back in the house with my wife and need to do a couple of things first, and I will be there as quickly as possible. So I went in and once again was employed by WCTC.

That was the first time I was fired. The final time, I stated on the air; they didn't pay me enough to take this abuse by a caller. I was the engineer for the Gary R' Nels talk show one Saturday afternoon, and I played a cart saying BORING, THIS CALL IS BORING, which I have in my possession for remembrance. The caller got upset with this and started to get upset with Gary.

Gary turned around and blamed me for this. I opened the mic and said they don't pay me enough to take this abuse from callers. It got around the station that I said this, and at the time, I was only getting 8 dollars an hour, and they were bringing new people for 10 dollars an hour. The funny thing was I was training these people and still made eight bucks an hour.

I also remember doing fabulous New Year's Eve Shows each year, which Tony Morano loved, and they gave me a quarter raise one year. He even left a quarter in my mailbox with a note to let me know. Anyway, these are some of the stories I can share, and the others we let go of for a much later time.

Bruce Johnson

I worked at WCTC for 34 years, beginning in 1980. I was the news and sports director for much of the period from 1986 to 2014. I grew up in Spotswood, New Jersey (about ten miles from where WCTC was located in New Brunswick at the time) as a New York City radio "snob", only listening to Top 40 radio on WABC and WMCA in the 1960s. I thought that was the beginning and end of all things radio until my fifth-grade teacher handed out postcards to our entire class. On the back were the call letters "WCTC" and the a-m radio frequency "1450." What caught my attention were the words, "Tune into 1450 WCTC every weekday morning when considerable snow is falling and find out whether your school had a snow day." What a concept! Tune into a radio station you never heard of and find out if you were off from school. So, I did that on snow-filled days. I turned on this 1450 radio station, discovering other signals at the opposite end of the dial from WMCA 570 and WABC 770. I quickly learned the drill that you had to wait for all the school closings in alphabetical order. That meant I had to wait a longgggg time to get to Spotswood and all the other school districts that began with the letter "S." But I waited and waited and often was rewarded when the announcer said, "Spotswood was off." It was like a Christmas gift from the radio. I was overjoyed when Spotswood was announced and envious of other schools when the announcer sent me to school, wondering why Woodbridge and Edison were so lucky that day.

After discovering WCTC for selfish reasons, I still listened faithfully to WMCA and WABC. But my mother became hooked on WCTC, listening on the kitchen radio to Central Jersey local news, weather, and the "middle of the road music" called "MOR." We're talking Frank Sinatra, Tony Bennett, Petula Clark, Barbra Streisand, and the like. All certainly a long cry from my favorites on the NYC radio signals that belted out the Beatles, Rolling Stones, Supremes, and the Four Seasons. But I still stopped and listened to WCTC while eating breakfast in the kitchen, finding something unique about a radio station in my "backyard" and talking about things in my "backyard." I also heard a man on WCTC with a great baritone voice who had the "gift of gab" but wasn't using the same Top 40 banter I heard on WMCA and WABC. He was engaging, provocative, and very smart about many topics. His name was

Jack Ellery, and he became one of the nationwide pioneers of local talk radio. But I came to find out that there was more to WCTC. There were other disc jockeys with dulcet tones like John Taylor, who hosted the afternoon drive program known as the "Raritan Roadshow," named after the Raritan River, which flowed through Middlesex County, with New Brunswick as the county seat. There were also the quirky elements of WCTC, including the hourly waiting times at the local Motor Vehicle inspection stations and the pollen counts from the local hospital. Then at night and on weekends, there were the broadcasts of Rutgers University (located in New Brunswick) football and basketball games and Central Jersey high school Games of the Week.

Even for a kid in my teens, I knew this was a vital radio station that catered to its Central Jersey audience. And it inspired me to get into broadcasting and to go to Ohio University to major in communications. In the summer of 1974, following my junior year in college, I was accepted to a news internship at WCTC. My exciting chance to get inside the doors of the downtown New Brunswick station influenced my career decision. My first time there in the early evening, I walked in with great anticipation and trepidation. Which "voice" would I bump into, and which person would acknowledge my existence? It wouldn't be Jack Ellery, who worked early mornings, but the news people I always heard on air and wanted to be a part of. In reality, they worked in a minimal office space, so small that the news recording booth was a closet. But I loved all of it that summer, sitting in the same room as all of the professional news people, including noted news director Walt Sodie, typing police stories from all the departments in Central Jersey, and going on outside assignments with a tape recorder and microphone that displayed a flag with the call letters "WCTC."

My summer quickly ended; I graduated the next year and began my professional career in suburban Cleveland, Ohio, but I always kept WCTC in mind. I wanted to return there because it epitomized local radio, and that atmosphere felt right. Eventually, I did get back there in 1980, a couple of years after the station moved to a beautiful new building in Somerset, on the outskirts of New Brunswick. I was hired by the legendary general manager Tony Marano to be part of the news team. After a stint in the Navy, Tony began as a news and sports announcer at WCTC in the late 1940s. He eventually became the play-by-play announcer for Rutgers and, quickly after that, was named the station's general manager. Much of what Tony did in that role was a blueprint for many general managers of the day. He was hands-on in almost every way. Tony was one of the first in the morning and the last in the evening. He coordinated the sales department's efforts, the station's financial lifeblood. Tony closely watched the news department product, the vital one-on-one connection with the Central Jersey audience. And he was an immeasurable presence at various local organizations and charities, representing WCTC in a way that made the station an integral part of the community. There aren't too many "Tony Marano's" in local radio because the industry is dominated by outside companies primarily interested in revenue, not in connections with the local areas they serve. Those of us who worked for many years for Tony used him as a guiding light on how to do local radio the "right way." We always tried to do what the Central

Jersey audience wanted and needed. We knew we differed from the 50,000-watt New York City station's mission statements like WABC. They were there for the masses, committed to making millions of dollars. We were for Central Jersey, committed to impacting the community.

Neil Solondz

My five and a half years at WCTC and WMGQ taught me so much that still helps me today. Not only were their great people to learn from, but some became life-long friends, and I stopped working for WCTC in early 2000.

Anyone who worked at WCTC was fortunate to have a tremendous teacher and mentor, first and foremost in Bruce Johnson. Bruce taught people how to prepare for the big picture and the day-to-day. No one settled for doing an excellent job because Bruce set such high standards. We also learned how to multi-task and handle deadlines. To anchor, report, and host a talk show on a typical day and continually go through seven-day work weeks, I learned the grind, a skill essential in eventually navigating an MLB season.

Bruce was a great teacher and terrific at recognizing talent. Gordon Deal is a national talk show host, and Jennifer Kushinka is a big part of his show. Rich DeMarco is the voice of Army Athletics. Marla Diamond and Peter Haskell are tremendous reporters and anchors at WCBS. They were among the many talented people to come through Bruce's door while I was there.

Yes, there were memorable days and unforgettable stories to cover. Three days with little or no sleep covering a two-and-a-half-foot snowstorm. Riding on a motorboat in downtown Bound Brook after flooding turned Main Street into a river. Handling a talk show from the RAC after a game was suspended at halftime when a sit-in halted the game. Finishing an overtime football game in a rare win over Syracuse when Bruce had to leave to catch a plan for a basketball game.

There were unforgettable athletes in their formative years, like eventual US Soccer goalie Tim Howard making big plays on the basketball court for North Brunswick High School. Or Shaheen Holloway playing long before his Cinderella run at St Peter's as a coach.

But the best memories involved were the terrific people we worked with each and every day. Every person in that newsroom had a kind heart and truly was about working for a team. We all succeeded in some regard, but there were no egos. I can't recall after the fourth-quarter comeback, but I remember all the fun times grabbing Chinese food with Gordon Deal after a high school football or basketball game.

What I remember most is how generous everyone was during a tough time. Long story short, in 1997 and 1998, my sister Debbie needed a bone marrow transplant for severe aplastic anemia, and I was her match. Each day, I worked at WCTC and drove into a hospital in New York City, spending the night there and repeating the cycle day after day.

None of us at that time were wealthy by any stretch, but it wasn't long after what turned out to be two months of commuting that at my workstation was a card with special notes from everyone in the department and cash collected to help pay for my tolls in and out of the city. You learn more about people during the most challenging times, and I saw what true friendship was about. WCTC was full of talented broadcasters but was made up of even better people.

Dave Marthouse

Keith Hill, the program director, interviewed me at WCTC/WMGQ in the summer of 1986. Keith liked my tape and resume and said my on-air style would fit WCTC.

At that time, WCTC was a "full-service station," which meant that the format and its music were a priority given to jocks with personality and strong community involvement. We were the flagship station for the Rutgers University Football and Basketball network. We also had an excellent local news and sports department led by Bruce Johnson.

Keith told me I would start in September after the new studio was done. I would be working with state-of-the-art equipment.

Since this was the mid-1980s, state-of-the-art broadcast equipment was primarily analog, consisting of consoles, turntables, tape recorders, CD players, and cart machines.

On the day I was scheduled to report for training and familiarization with the equipment, I met Tony DeNicola, Aka Tony Dee, who would later become a pivotal part of my future broadcast career, but I am getting ahead of my story.

As a blind person, I had to do a few things that were different from the standard way a sighted broadcaster would work,

I would bring a braille typewriter to write the program log for my air shift. This gave me an outline of what program elements ran at specific times, commercials, public service announcements, and other show-related items. In addition, I had the music on file cards in braille and their corresponding numbers relating to the carts on which each program element was recorded.

Other than the above, I did everything else that my sited counterparts did in doing a radio program.

As well as doing on-air work, I recorded commercials in the production room.
A few years later, we became an affiliate of the Westwood I Radio Network and carried TalkNet featuring such radio luminaries as Bruce Williams (a WCTC alumnus), Neal Mires, Dara Wells, and a host of others.

As the calendar flipped to the early '90s, WCTC transitioned from a "Full Service" music, news, and talk station to primarily talking. In addition to my duties, running the board for TalkNet, and doing production, I became a local talk show host.

One particular event from this period stands out. The Texas Eastern Transmission Corporation Natural Gas Pipeline Explosion and Fire occurred in Edison, New Jersey, on March 23, 1994. Where a natural gas pipeline broke and exploded into flames next to the Durham Woods apartment complex along New Durham Road at its junction with Interstate 287.

The NTSB gave the cause of this breakage as mechanical damage caused by a backhoe that gauged out 1/4" of steel off the pipe. This was done on a property adjacent to the complex.[2] The resulting fire destroyed or severely damaged 14 of the apartment buildings. Over 1,500 apartment residents were evacuated, 125 residential apartments, and nine complete buildings, were killed, and their occupants were left homeless. Miraculously, no one died as a direct result of the explosion.

I was on the air that night. At around 1230 in the morning, I heard what sounded like a clap of thunder. This was an unusual occurrence, to say the least, as our studios were soundproof.

About 30 seconds later, every publicly known phone line in our studios rang at once. It frightened listeners calling us to find out what happened.

Then the hotline rang. It was Bruce Johnson. He told me to interrupt TalkNet and go on air, taking calls from the audience to get a handle on what was happening.

In the meantime, Bruce and our entire news department were on their way in. I went on air and started taking the calls while Bruce and the news department went into action. Bruce and I anchored the broadcast all night, with me taking calls while receiving periodic updates from the newsroom.

We must have taken at least a thousand calls from concerned listeners throughout the night. When my shift ended and the morning show with Jack Ellery started, the call volume hadn't stopped. It was an unforgettable experience and a baptism of fire for me as a news/talk host.

Many of us in the radio business dream of owning our radio station.
This happened to me in 1995. Tony Dee, who trained me initially when I joined the station, approached me with an idea.

He was looking through Radio World (a broadcasting trade journal) and saw an ad for a small radio station for sale in Brookneal, Virginia. He asked me if I was interested in looking at it out of curiosity.

We took the trip to rural Virginia, and to make a long story short, we eventually bought WODI and put the distressed station back on the air.

After ten years, I left WCTC/WMGQ to go to Virginia to run the station as President and General Manager. Tony and I still associate as business partners and close friends. We ran WODI for almost 14 years till we sold it.

Without the invaluable experiences I had working for WCTC, I wouldn't have been able to move on and realize my dream as a radio station owner.

The Photo Gallery

The fulltime six-man WCTC news team is the largest radio broadcast news operation in the state. Preparing some 30 newscasts each day keeps them busy and on the go, but they are dedicated to delivering timely and accurate news on the local, county, state, national and international level.

WCTC's advertising staff consists of experienced Account Executives and creative copywriters who work closely with advertisers to produce effective and informative commercials.

ANTHONY (TONY) MARANO

Known throughout the Central Jersey area as "Tony" and as the "Voice of Rutgers Sports", the General Manager of WCTC has spent all of his life in the area served by the station.

Tony joined the staff as a part-time sports reporter while still attending Rider College. After receiving his degree in Journalism and Commerce, he became a full-time member of the WCTC News Department.

As the Central Jersey community grew, Tony grew with it, advancing from Sports Reporter to Newsman to News Director to Assistant Station Manager to General Manager, which position he has held since 1965.

Despite the many demands made upon his time by station business, Tony still finds time for participation in many community service projects and for his role as the "Voice of Rutgers Sports." He calls his role as the Rutgers play-by-play man the "fun" part of his job.

Through his involvement in community affairs, Tony is able to keep his finger on the pulse of the Central Jersey area, which he feels results in programming responsive to the needs of the community.

The WCTC announcing staff represents more than 70 years of broadcasting experience. As active workers in community affairs, they are interested in the people of Central Jersey and know what WCTC's listeners want to hear in the way of music and information.

The production facilities at the WCTC studios are in operation continually as engineers prepare and edit tapes, record public service announcements, weather forecasts and program features for broadcast.

…and the Stars Pay WCTC a Visit

Bela Lagosi

Bruce Williams

Mickey Ronney

Elmo the Clown Clowns Around with Jack Ellery While Appearing as

A Guest on Jack's Morning Show

WCTC Air Personality Scott Lawrence and Community Affairs Director

Lee Robinson Greet Tweety Bird During a Halloween Visit

…WCTC Spends Nearly a Third of Its Broadcast Time on The Road.

At Remotes, Appearances, and Sporting Events!

Here Are Some Examples!

WCTC's New Director Bruce Johnson at The Scene of An Explosion and Fire at The Chemray Coating Plant in Central Jersey. Hundreds Of People in The Area Had to Be Evacuated, and The Station Assisted the Local Police and Fire Departments with News Reports Throughout the Day.

Mike Jarmus At the Middlesex County Fair

Buddy Seibert on the Road

WCTC In Jamesburg for The Arrival of Santa Clause!

Steve Tapper On Location

Mike Jarmus Looking Sharp in The WCTC Blazer

Mike Jarmus Broadcasting from An Exotic Location on The Lawn Outside of WCTC Studios

**WCTC Always Had Time
for A Parade**

WCTC Tony Dee Hands Out Prizes at A Remote

WCTC Air Personality Jack Ellery Interviews Governor Thomas Kean During

Grand Opening Festivities at the Hyatt Regency Hotel.

Listeners Win Girl Scout Cookies and Other Premiums Just for Listeners to

WCTC 1450 AM

Each Year Around Valentine's Day, WCTC-AM, New Brunswick, NJ, Turns Its Offices and Studios Over to The American Heart Association

for the Annual Radiothon. The Station Has Raised More Than $600,00

Since the inception of "Operation Heartbeat"

23 Years Ago.

WCTC-AM, New Brunswick, NJ, Air Personality Scott Lawrence (wearing the sunglasses)
Handles the Radio Promotion and Volunteer Recruitment for the

March of Dimes Annual Walkathon

Mid-Day Personality Mike Jarmus and Morning Show Host Jack Ellery Appear to be Bad Broadcasters, and We Had to Call in the Law. It's the Annual Cancer Society Jail-A-Thon. WCTC-AM, New Brunswick, NJ, has Promoted This event For Numerous Years.

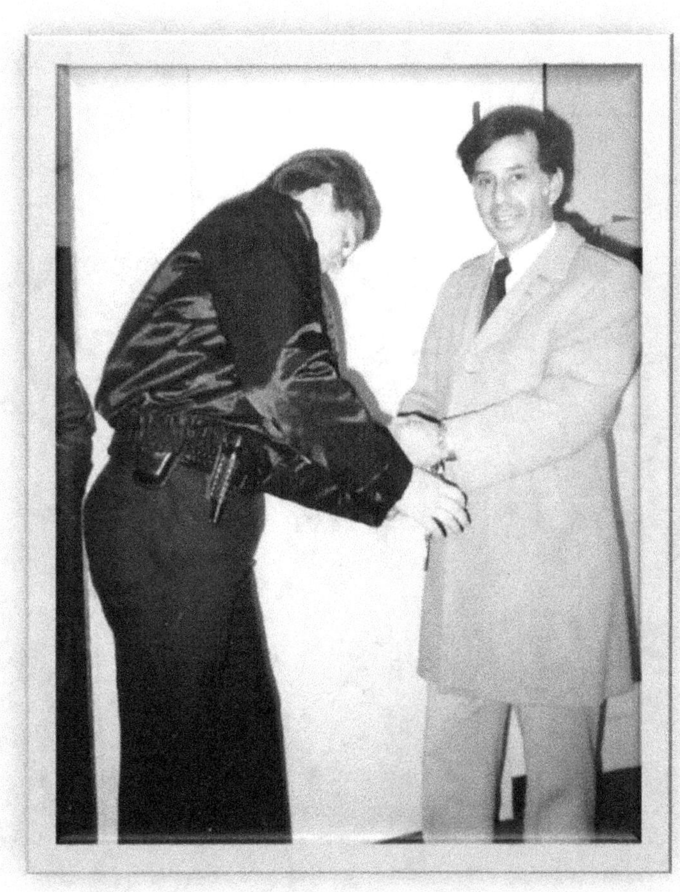

WCTC Bruce Johnson Presents Annual High School Basketball Award to Winning Carteret High School Coach Bill Karatz and Players Keith Huse and Corey Lowe.

WCTC Bruce Johnson Presents Gift to Rutgers Lady Knights Basketball Coach Theresa Grentz

WCTC's Jack Ellery at Somerset Studios in Crush the Orange Promotion/Before Rutgers 1991 Meeting with Syracuse. The Rutgers Cheerleaders and the Ladies from Bazooka's were in Attendance.

WCTC Sports Director Bruce Johnson and Former Giant's QB Scott Brunner, Along with Buddy Seibert, at the WCTC Tailgate Party in 1991 For Rutgers Football.

WCTC Operations Manager Jack Shreve Takes Contest Winners to the Ballgame at Yankee Stadium.

…WCTC a Winning Team for Decades Serving Central New Jersey… For More Than 40 Years, WCTC Has Served the Middlesex, Somerset, and Surrounding Counties with Entertainment News/Talk and Local Central Jersey Information!

THE WINNING TEAM 1989
National Association of
NAB
BROADCASTERS
THE CRYSTAL RADIO AWARDS
for excellence in local achievement
WCTC-AM
New Brunswick, NJ

WCTC Operations Manager, General Manager Tony Marano, Jack Shreve, and WMGQ PD Joe DeRose With Awards for Public Service Programming and Best Commercial

New Jersey Broadcasters Association

ANNUAL STATION AWARD
BEST PUBLIC AFFAIRS

1986

to

"THE DAY THE MARTIANS LANDED"

MIKE JARMUS, DON SMITH
& JOHN WEBER

WCTC
New Brunswick

40th ANNUAL N J B A CONVENTION
SEPTEMBER 29, 1986

WCTC New Brunswick Programming Is Always Aimed at Helping and Informing Our Central Jersey Listeners. In Doing So, WCTC Receives Many Honors,

For Employees Dedication!

Jack Shreve Operations Manager

Peggy Graffin and Traffic Manager Joann Nolan

WCTC Morning Show

Producer Ed Palladino

Dane Lowrie WCTC/WMGQ Copy Chief

Since 1947 Peter Kara Has Broadcast the Hungarian Melody Time Program Sunday Afternoons!

WCTC Most Treasured Possession!!

Ralph Savino, Mid-Day Wednesday Money Line Show

Home and Garden Expert and Mid-Day Friday Hostess, Peggy Ballister-Howells

WCTC News/Sports Director and The Voice of Rutgers Football & Basketball,

Bruce Johnson

Liz Maita WCTC Air Personality, Heard Each Saturday Afternoon

…Where the Magic Happened

WCTC Main Studio

WCTC Talk Studio

WCTC Newsroom

WCTC Lobby